AF450013

Falco Tarassaco

PROPHECIES OF THE END TIMES

CENTURIES OF YESTERDAY
QUATRAINS OF TODAY

DAMANHUR

Falco Tarassaco

PROPHECIES OF THE END TIMES

ISBN 978-88-941-185-4-4

Ist English edition (Ist Italian edition *Edizioni Horus 1980*)

Devodama srl - 10080 Vidracco (TO) - Italy

Printed in May 2016

Our thanks to Beira and David Sutcliffe for the translation and Ape Soia for the illustration on the cover.

CONTENTS

PREFACE

In 1980, Falco Tarassaco, Oberto Airaudi, the founder of Damanhur, published this book of prophecies for the first time, bringing together the quatrains which had already been appearing monthly in the newsletter of the Centro Horus, the Centre out of which the Federation of Communities subsequently came.

The universe speaks to us through its own formations, through its "being", which includes the forms that populate this universe (ranging from those we perceive through our five senses to those we perceive through our intuition) together with time. Time exists in the universe – or at least in our universe, the Universe of Forms, the only one we have experience of – like a temporal sea. Here all the ages and thus all possible events, are simultaneously present. Whoever is able to listen to the universe can turn its voice into so many images. Or prophecies.

A prophecy states the possible scenarios that may await us; on the one hand to prepare us for them and on the other to show how intricately interconnected are the threads of time – so much so that we are able to foresee events, if only in allegorical form.

It is perhaps this which brings all prophecies closest to our daily lives: they remind us of the "circular" dimension of space and time where, more than chronology or the reading of cause and effect, what counts is the angle from which we observe events amid the laws governing the universe.

To better understand the frame of reference in which to interpret Falco Tarassaco's prophecies, we need to consider the theory of the separation of the planes which constitutes one of the keys to interpretation that he put forward to bring his message into focus.

Falco explains that by the middle of the third Millennium, planet Earth will have arrived at a situation where life is unsustainable owing to the deterioration of the environment and the impoverishment of spiritual values.

The Galactic Council, which watches over the evolution of life, decides to send a being to Earth, six hundred years back into the past, entrusted with the task of creating new conditions for survival and a new plane of reality, separate from the one that had "already happened". Consequently, today, the whole of humanity lives on a plane of existence which is both real and virtual, the purpose being to densify this alternative plane so that it can substitute the previous one.

In this new sequence of time, which has just begun, there is the figure of Falco Tarassaco, there is Damanhur with all its developments, you and the book which you are now reading.

I refer the reader to the last section of the book for a critical analysis of Prophecies of the End Times *and their representing a message of hope to project into the future, despite those "end times".*

Cigno Banano

In translating Falco's quatrains we made a consistent effort to keep closely to his original version, trying to mirror his poetic style in rhyme as well as in rhythm. Luckily, we were able to find full rhyming in almost half of the 123 quatrains (either ABAB as chosen by Falco, or AABB) and a single rhyme in all the others but five. In practically all of the quatrains, as translated by us, there is a good poetic rhythm which defines them as poetry in any case. Needless to say, we would welcome and encourage any suggestions to improve the rhymes in our version. This poetic version is complemented by a more literal translation in prose of Falco's text on the facing page.

David Sutcliffe & Beira

FOREWORD

As clearly expressed in the title, we are talking of prophecies of the end times that unfortunately (or finally), are very, very near.

In fact, all the prophecies, those of Nostradamus, of the Black Spider of the Great Pyramid etc., agree on the years of a future catastrophic event in a way which is truly striking and these times are now upon us. We are arriving at one of the cyclical moments, a day of reckoning for the human race.

Plato, in the *Timaeus*, hands down what was said by the priest of Sais to Solon:

"O Solon, you Greeks are little boys and there is no old Greek among you. You are of childish minds, all of you. Why is it that you have never heard any ancient opinions, not even in science which has been of age for a long time?

And this is why: many times and in many ways there has been and there will be the destruction of Humankind and it will happen again by means of fire and water." [...]

"Here once more, after the normal passing of years, like an illness raging down, will come floods from the sky, leaving you rough and illiterate, so that you are always starting all over again like beginners, knowing nothing of what had happened in ancient times." [...]

"You only remember a single cataclysm of the Earth, whereas there have been many. When such disturbances of the celestial movements happen at long intervals new general configurations necessarily follow."

Above, alongside the word 'unfortunately', referring obviously to the serious distress and the great suffering that will accompany the near future, it says 'or finally'; finally because this will mark the beginning of a New Era, of a New Humankind. A Humankind of the Age of Aquarius.

A Humankind conscious of its strength and value, of its role on this planet where it knows how to live in symbiosis with the true Reality of all that surrounds it; conscious of being part of a whole in continuous harmonious evolution, conscious of the power of maya for which it will have the key.

This key which opens all doors is called Love, with a capital 'L' of course. All human beings will be aware of the brilliant destiny that awaits them and to make this come true they will act with all their strength, all their enthusiasm, all their Being. They will have to do this if they want and know how to avoid the errors that they had committed in this last Kali Yuga, exalting and adoring the false gods 'Ego' and 'Pride' and crucifying the real God 'Unconditional-Love'.

PROPHECIES
OF THE END TIMES

(1)

THOSE YEARS WHOSE FACTORS' SUM
GIVES A NUMBER LESS BY ONE THAN
THE LAST FIGURE OF THE YEAR'S NUMBER
WILL BE YEARS WHEN GREAT CRISES COME.

(2)

FROM THE YEAR WHOSE FACTORS' SUM
GIVES A NUMBER WHICH IS IDENTICAL QUITE
TO THE LAST FIGURE, THERE WILL BEGIN
THE YEARS OF CATASTROPHE,
BUT ALSO OF THE HOPE OF AQUARIUS.

(3)

FROM THE YEAR WHOSE FACTORS' SUM
GIVES A NUMBER WHICH IS GREATER BY ONE
THAN THE LAST FIGURE, THERE WILL BE
NO TIME TO THINK OF CATASTROPHE,
SINCE ALL THAT WAS CONCEIVED WILL HAVE BEGUN.

PROPHECIES OF THE END TIMES

(1)

THOSE YEARS THE SUM OF WHOSE FACTORS
GIVES A NUMBER ONE LESS THAN
THE LAST DIGIT OF THE YEAR'S NUMBER
WILL BE YEARS OF GREAT CRISES.

(2)

FROM THE YEAR WHOSE FACTORS' SUM
IS IDENTICAL QUITE TO ITS LAST DIGIT
WILL BEGIN YEARS OF CATASTROPHE
BUT ALSO OF THE HOPE OF AQUARIUS.

(3)

FROM THE YEAR WHOSE FACTORS' SUM
IS GREATER BY ONE THAN ITS LAST DIGIT
THERE WILL BE NO TIME TO THINK OF CATASTROPHE
SINCE ALL THAT WAS CONCEIVED WILL HAVE BEGUN.

(4)

WATERS LOW, WATERS HIGH,
FIRE AND THIRTY MONTHS
THAT IMPRISONED IN THE CASES
FEW FULL LENGTH CAN LIE.

(5)

FROM THE SEA WITHOUT A LEADER
THE ARMIES OF THE HUNGRY CLAMBER
SCREAMS CRUEL, FINALLY SHOTS AND CRIES
A NUMBER IN THE MILLIONS DIES.

(6)

THE MIDDLE AGES RETURN AND WILL BE BRUTAL
THE CITIES SPENT, STARVATION,
WITH ONLY CANDLES FOR ILLUMINATION
COPPER THE ONLY CRAFTED METAL.

(4)

WATERS HIGH, WATERS LOW,
FIRE AND THIRTY MONTHS
THAT CLOSED IN THE CASES
ONLY A FEW WILL LIE STRETCHED OUT.

(5)

FROM THE SEA THEY COME UNLED
ARMIES OF THE HUNGRY
SCREAMS CRUEL, FINALLY SHOTS AND CRIES
BY THE MILLIONS THEY ARE DECIMATED.

(6)

THE MIDDLE AGES RETURN AND IT WILL BE CRUEL
THE CITIES LIFELESS, HUNGER,
ONLY LIGHTS ARE CANDLES
THE ONLY METAL WORKED, COPPER.

(7)

A GREAT CLEANSING OF THE EARTH
A GREAT WASHING OF PAVED WAYS
THE WAVE THAT CANCELS ALSO WAR
RISES SWIFT AND IN AN INSTANT SLAYS.

(8)

THE EASTERN STARS ARE ALL A-QUIVER
TURNING PALLID BEFORE A TAIL
VIOLET IS THE EARTH, AND ALL A-SHIVER,
GNAWED AS BY A GOD, SEE IT CRUMBLE, FAIL.

(9)

AN ENTIRE YEAR APPEARS AND STAYS
AS OF YORE IN ANCIENT DAYS
SHAKEN ARE THE PEOPLE, BUT YET
THE FOLK NOW RISE WHOSE SKIN IS JET.

(7)

A GREAT CLEANSING ON EARTH
A GREAT WASHING OF ITS FLOOR
THE WAVE THAT CANCELS ALSO WAR
RISES QUICKLY AND SMASHES DOWN IN AN INSTANT.

(8)

THE STARS ALL TREMBLE IN THE EAST
TURNING PALE IN FRONT OF A TAIL
VIOLET IS THE EARTH, AND ALL TREMBLES,
BREAKS UP, COLLAPSES AS IF A GOD GNAWS IT.

(9)

AN ENTIRE YEAR APPEARS AND STOPS
AND AS ALREADY IN PAST MILLENNIA
SHAKES THE PEOPLE AND MAKES THE HEAD ERECT
PARTICULARLY THOSE OF THE BLACK PEOPLES.

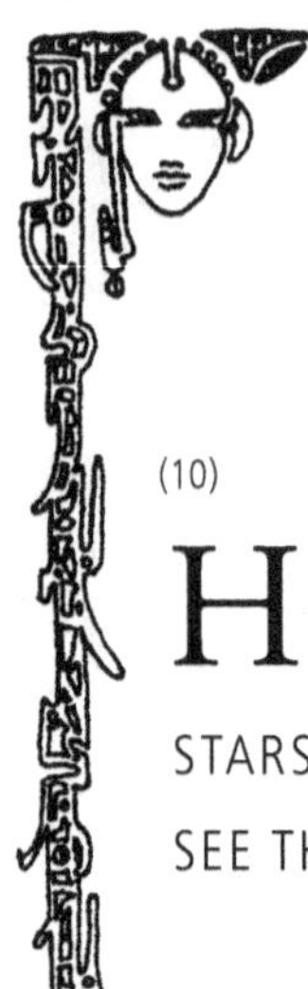

(10)

Humankind anchors in the skies
But it is difficult there to dwell
Stars and demon watched unveiled
See them return to make all unwell.

(11)

The madness rife in every being
Hot and cold reversed, all altered
The bird migrates and man, fearful, follows
Trampling those whom he has slaughtered.

(12)

New earthquakes and a new island bursts
Emerging from the sea through steam and fire,
Who, crazed, discovers it first
Sign of the first people their final ire.

(10)

HUMANKIND ANCHORS SHIPS IN THE SKY
BUT IT IS DIFFICULT TO STAY THERE
STARS AND DEMON WATCHED WITHOUT VEIL
BEHOLD, THEY RETURN TO AFFLICT US.

(11)

MADNESS IN EVERY CREATURE
HOT AND COLD ARE REVERSED
THE BIRD MIGRATES AND THE MAN WHO FEARS
FOLLOWS AND TRAMPLES THOSE HE HAS KILLED.

(12)

NEW EARTHQUAKES AND A NEW ISLAND
APPEARS OUT OF THE SEA THROUGH FIRE AND STEAM
WHOEVER, CRAZY, FIRST DISCOVERS IT
SIGNALS THE LAST FURY OF THE FIRST PEOPLE.

(13)

AFTER THIRTY MONTHS THE NEW AGE DAWNS
AND THE FISH HAVE FLED FROM AQUARIUS
ALL OF NATURE ITSELF RESPAWNS
AND FROM THE EARTH, O NEW MAN, COME!

(14)

FRESHLY SPRINGING, SEE NEW GRASS START
AND MANY AN ANIMAL RETURNING
IF MANKIND NO LONGER LOSES ITS PURE HEART
AND THE DEMONS ARE RECEDING.

(15)

IN THE REMADE SKY THIS NOW IS BUT A DOT
NOW SO FAR AWAY AND MINDS ARE SANE
THE SKY BEING MILKED OF ITS TEEMING RAIN
O'ER THE PASTURES NEW, AND BREAD ALREADY GOT.

(13)

AFTER THIRTY MONTHS IT IS THE NEW ERA
AND FROM AQUARIUS PISCES IS GONE
ALL OF NATURE IS RENEWED
AND FROM THE EARTH, O NEW MAN, COME!

(14)

THE NEW GREEN GRASS BREAKS THROUGH
AND MANY ANIMALS RETURN
IF ITS PURE HEART MANKIND NO LONGER LOSES
AND THE DEMONS HAVE LEFT.

(15)

IN THE REMADE SKY NOW IT IS ONLY A POINT
IT MOVES FAR AWAY AND MINDS ARE SANE
MANY THE RAINS, THE SKY HAS BEEN MILKED
IN THE NEW FIELDS BREAD ALREADY GROWS.

(16)

THERE ARE INSECTS IN NUMBER SOVEREIGN
AND THE NEAREST MOON HAS SHONE
ON THE ROUGH DANGER IN THE GRAIN
YET HUMANKIND WILL RULE, BUT WITH A THORN!

(17)

THE NEW MEN THAT TO THE YOUNG WILL SAY
HOW THE WORLD WAS UPON A DAY
TO THOSE INCREDULOUS THEY WILL SHOW
MEMORIES AND DRAWINGS WIPED OUT A TIME AGO.

(18)

THE TOIL IS HARD AND HARD THE FRAY
BUT MEMORIES AND THE SCIENCE ARE CONSERVATED
BECAUSE UPON A DAY SOMEONE WILL TELL
HOW LOOMS, ROPE AND STEAM WERE ALL CREATED.

(16)

THE INSECTS ARE IN SOVEREIGN NUMBER
AND THE NEAREST MOON ILLUMINATES
THE ROUGH DANGER ON THE GRAIN
BUT HUMANKIND WILL RULE, WITH A THORN!

(17)

THE NEW MEN THAT TO THE YOUNG WILL SAY
HOW THE WORLD WAS IN TIMES PAST
TO THOSE INCREDULOUS THEY WILL SHOW
THE MEMORIES AND THE CANCELLED DRAWINGS.

(18)

THE FIGHT IS HARD AND HARD IS THE TOIL
BUT PRESERVE THE MEMORIES AND THE SCIENCE
SO THAT ONE DAY SOMEONE CAN SAY
HOW THE LOOMS, ROPE AND STEAM WERE BORN.

(19)

EVERY CONQUEST IS THE WORK OF ALL
THE HOUSES, TEMPLE, FIELDS AND HIVES
THE BROW NOW SMOOTH, THE BAD TIMES GONE
MEMORY AND BITTER DREAMS WILL LINGER ON.

(20)

ENVY AND CRISIS HAVE MOVED FAR AFIELD
NOURISHED BY TOIL AND STRONG COMMAND
UNITED STRONG, WITH WINGS UNFURLED
FROM FLIGHT PLANE RIDING DOWN TO LAND.

(21)

THE ART OF HEALING UNITES THOSE FOLK
AND A NEW PEOPLE IT HAS WROUGHT
STRONG THE DEFENCE WHERE WINDS WAIL
AND THE INVADER LURKING STILL IS BUT A TALE.

(19)

EVERY CONQUEST IS THE WORK OF ALL
THE HOUSES, THE TEMPLE, THE FIELDS AND THE BEEHIVES
THE BROW IS SMOOTH THE BAD TIMES DISTANT
MEMORIES, BITTER DREAMS, REMAIN.

(20)

ENVY AND CRISES HAVE MOVED AWAY
NOURISHED BY TOIL AND STRONG COMMAND
UNITED STRONG, WITH WINGS OUTSTRETCHED
FROM THE PLANE OF FLIGHT RIDING DOWN.

(21)

THE ART OF HEALING UNITES THE PEOPLES
AND A NEW PEOPLE IT HAS BUILT;
STRONG DEFENCE WHERE THERE ARE WINDS
AND THE INVADER REMAINING IS A MYTH.

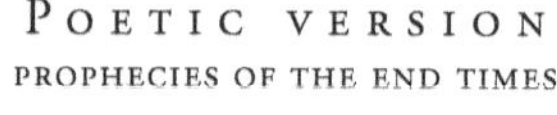

(22)

F IRE AND WATER, CLUBS AND ARROWS ARE DEPLOYED
WHEN A HORDE OF MARCHING MICE APPEARS
GONE ARE THE BEASTIES AND ALL THE BARK DESTROYED,
AND COURAGE REMAINS THROUGH MANY TEARS.

(23)

S O HIGH THE SNOW THAT PLAINS ARE MADE OF VALLEYS
THE ROOFS COLLAPSING DOWN AND FROST BINDS
ENTERING THE BODIES BY A THOUSAND CRANNIES
THE SECOND WINTER PAST, PURE ARE THE MINDS.

(24)

T HE JOURNEY AND DISCOVERY OF THE EXPLORER DARK
THE MINDS OF COMMAND DECIDING
AMID REEKING SMOKE ALL FOLK REMAINING
PREPARE THE JOURNEY AND THEN EMBARK.

(22)

FIRE AND WATER AND STICKS AND ARROWS
FOR THE ARMY OF MIGRANT MICE
THE BEASTS AND THE BARK DESTROYED
COURAGE REMAINS THROUGH MANY TEARS.

(23)

SO HIGH THE SNOW THAT VALLEYS BECOME PLAINS
THE ROOFS COLLAPSE TO THE GROUND AND THE FROST
ENTERS IN THE BODIES BY A THOUSAND CRACKS
THE SECOND WINTER PAST AND PURE ARE THE MINDS.

(24)

THE JOURNEY AND THE DISCOVERY OF THE BROWN EXPLORER
THE MINDS OF COMMAND DECIDE
ALL THE PEOPLE REMAINED, IN THE MIDST OF THE SMOKE
PREPARE THE JOURNEY AND EMIGRATE.

(25)

FOLLOWING THE FALCON DOWN THE EARTH
THE NEW NORTH IS SHIFTED FAR AWAY
BY THE NATURAL BRIDGE A GREENHOUSE THRIVES,
AND THE WEARY PEOPLE STAY.

(26)

NEW HOUSES AND RICH VILLAGES
FOOD AND WEALTH BUT LET THE HEART BE PURE
THERE REMAINS THE RULE DELEGATED TO THE SAGES
AND NE'ER RETURNS THE IMMENSE HARDNESS TO ENDURE.

(27)

IN LATTER YEARS THE ICE AND SNOW
ON THE NATIONS THAT LEAD THE WEST,
THE DEAD IN DIRE ICE-COLD PALACES LIE,
STATES AND CAPITALS SNOW-BURIED WITH THE REST.

(25)

FOLLOWING THE FALCON THE EARTH DESCENDS
THE NEW NORTH IS GREATLY SHIFTED
BY THE NATURAL BRIDGE THERE IS A THRIVING GREENHOUSE
AND THE TIRED PEOPLE HAVE STOPPED.

(26)

NEW HOUSES AND WEALTHY VILLAGES
FOOD, WEALTH BUT MAY THE HEART BE PURE
AND THE COMMAND DELEGATED TO THE WISE
AND NEVER MORE THE IMMENSE HARSHNESS RETURNS.

(27)

IN THE LATTER YEARS ICE AND SNOW
ON THE NATIONS THAT THE WEST LEADS
DEAD IN THE COLD IN THE BUILDINGS DIRE
STATES AND CAPITALS BURIED WITH PEOPLE.

(28)

IN THE ITALIAN BOOT, AN OLDEN SWAMP,
THE EARTH QUIVERS AND LAND SLIDES
DRIES UP AND WITHOUT RAIN A YEAR ABIDES
EVERY WOUND RE-OPENED IS THEN SEALED
BUT WINTER AGAIN SUMMONS UP THE SNOW
AT CHRISTMAS IT SHIFTS AGAIN, WITH UNTOLD WOE.

(29)

ALL THE WORLD WANTS OIL FROM THE GROUND
POSSESSED BY THE PEOPLES OF THE SANDS
IN A THOUSAND PRETEXTS HIDDEN WARS ABOUND
AND BLOOD IS SPILT AND POURS FROM VEINS.

(30)

FROM ON HIGH THE FIRE COMES AND GOES
FROM BELOW THE FIRE UPWARD GROWS
AND FROM MOUNTAINS LIKE BAKING BREAD
UPON THE WINDMILL SAILS A HOT WIND BLOWS.

(28)

IN THE (ITALIAN) BOOT, OLD SWAMP,

THE EARTH TREMBLES AND COLLAPSES

DRIED UP AND WITHOUT RAIN ONE YEAR

EVERY WOUND RE-OPENS AND CLOSES

BUT WINTER, WITH HIGH SNOW, CALLS

AT CHRISTMAS IT SLIPS AGAIN, SO GREAT DAMAGE.

(29)

ALL THE WORLD REQUIRES THE OIL OF THE EARTH

THAT THE MAN OF THE SAND HOLDS

AMONG A THOUSAND EXCUSES WAR IS CONCEALED

BLOOD IS SPILT AND POURS FROM THE VEINS.

(30)

FROM ON HIGH THE FIRE GOES AND RETURNS

FROM BELOW THE FIRE RISES

FROM THE MOUNTAINS LIKE BREAD FROM THE OVEN

AND WIND BLOWS HOT ON THE BLADES.

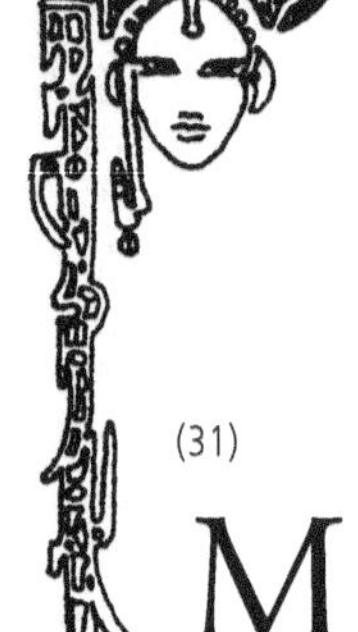

(31)

MIGRATING BIRDS ARE TWICE RETURNING
IN ONE YEAR, DEATH AND NEW ILLNESS VILE
THE GREEN LEAVES APLENTY FALLING
MUTE, THE BLIND ANIMAL HOWLS: SO MANY TRIALS!

(32)

MANY IN TWO DAYS GO BLIND
SINCE NEW COLOURS THERE ARE GALORE
LIKE OVENS ARE THE MINDS OF ALL MANKIND
MANY THE SUICIDES AND PAINS ARE SORE.

(33)

FROM THE SEA THERE COMES A WALL-WAVE,
AND FRIENDS THEIR FRIENDS WILL SLAUGHTER
THE TALLEST BUILDINGS ARE A GRAVE
AND WHAT SURVIVES IS CHANCE — THE WIND'S LAUGHTER.

(31)

THE BIRDS MIGRATE AND RETURN TWICE
IN THE SAME YEAR DEATHS AND NEW ILLNESSES
THE LEAVES THAT FALL GREEN ARE MANY
SCREAMS THE BLIND ANIMAL WITHOUT VOICE:
HOW MANY TRIALS!

(32)

MANY BLIND IN TWO DAYS
SO MANY ARE THE NEW COLOURS
THE MINDS OF ALL ARE OVENS
MANY SUICIDES AND GREAT PAIN.

(33)

A WALL COMES FROM THE SEA
FRIEND KILLS FRIEND
THE HIGHEST BUILDINGS ARE COFFINS
WHAT REMAINS DOES SO BY CHANCE, THE WIND LAUGHS.

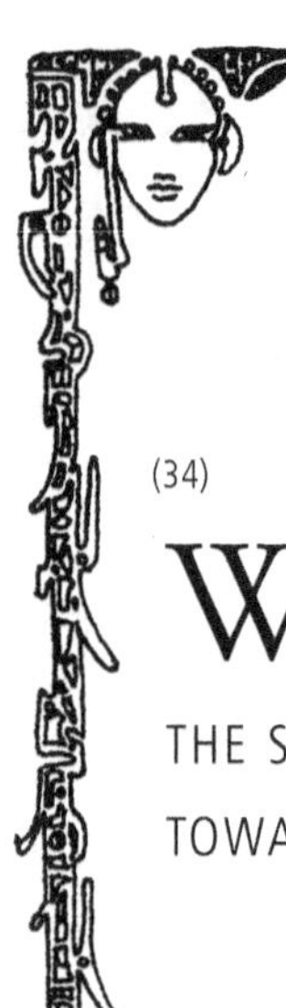

(34)

WATER NOW MEETS WITH FIRE
AND PEOPLE GASP FOR AIR
THE SHIPS' CREWS TURNED MUTINEERS
TOWARD THE PALACE THE HELM STEERS.

(35)

SHIPS COAST ALONG A NEW INDENTED SHORE
HERE BELOW A CITY STOOD THEY SAY
THE WATERS, NOW, ARE PURE ONCE MORE
AND MEMORIES OF OTHER ERAS FADE AWAY.

(36)

CALM MOUNTAINS BECOME VOLCANOES
AND FROM THE SKY THREE ROCKS LIKE HOUSES FALL
ARCANE QUESTIONS WORRIEDLY ARE POSED
BEFORE THE LANDS ARE INVADED ALL.

(34)

WATER AND FIRE MET
ALREADY THE PEOPLE CANNOT BREATHE
THE CREWS HAVE MUTINIED
TOWARDS THE PALACE THE HELM IS TURNED.

(35)

SHIPS COAST ALONG NEW INLETS
HERE BELOW, THEY SAY, THERE WAS A CITY
THE WATERS, NOW, ARE PURE AGAIN
THE MEMORIES OF OTHER ERAS HAVE FADED.

(36)

CALM MOUNTAINS BECOME VOLCANOES
FROM THE SKY THREE ROCKS LIKE HOUSES
ALL, DISTRESSED, QUESTIONING THE ARCANE
BEFORE THE LANDS ARE INVADED.

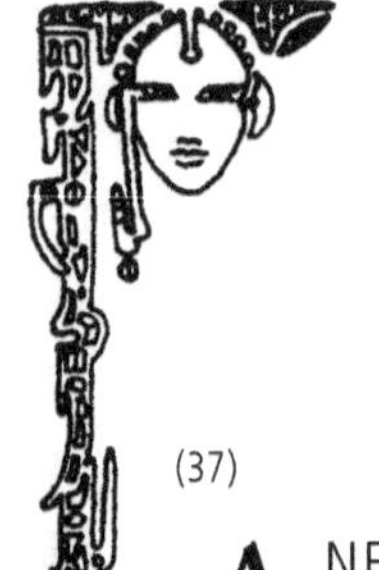

(37)

A NEW SAN ANDREAS FAULT DIVIDES
THE LAND AND BREAKS UP A RIVER
THE GREAT CURRENT CHANGES ALSO TIDES
BIRDS FEATHERLESS, MEN BORN WITH FEATHERS.

(38)

A CHURCH OPENS
LIKE SEGMENTS OF AN ORANGE PEELED
THIS IS THE TIME OF SOUR AND OVER-RIPENED FRUIT
AN ANCIENT CITY IS REVEALED
WHERE WRITING SEEMS SPEARS
IN THE SKY DARK CLOUDS ALL ABOUT.

(39)

ALL THE IMAGES ARE STAINED
BUT YET MACHINES ARE STILL INTACT
STRANGE DESIGNS UPON THE CREATURES BORN
CLOUDS UPON THE MOUNTAINS FORM A VASTER TRACT.

(37)

A NEW SAN ANDREAS FAULT
DIVIDES A LAND AND BREAKS UP A RIVER
CHANGES THE GREAT CURRENT AND THE TIDE
BIRDS WITHOUT, MAN BORN WITH FEATHERS.

(38)

A CHURCH IS OPENED
LIKE THE SEGMENTS OF AN ORANGE
IT IS THE TIME OF SOUR AND RIPE FRUIT
ANCIENT CITY DISCOVERED
WHERE THE WRITING IS LIKE SPEARS
IN THE SKY HUGE DARK CLOUDS.

(39)

ALL THE IMAGES ARE STAINED
BUT THE MACHINES ARE NOT BROKEN
STRANGE DESIGNS ON THE NEWBORN CREATURES
ON THE MOUNTAINS THE CLOUDS ARE MUCH VASTER.

(40)

ON THE SUN IS SEEN WITH NAKED SIGHT
THE LARGEST BLACK WEAL
SEE OSIRIS FROM HIS CHARIOT ALIGHT
WHILE ISIS RISES, MUCH MORE REAL.

(41)

THE MARBLE MELTS IN THE HEAT
AND IN THE COLD LIKE WAX
THE HEAD FROM THE STABLE THORAX
SLIDES, CONTINUES IN THE DARKLING NIGHT.

(42)

THE SWEET WATER IS ALL DEFILED
IN ONE DAY AS IN WAR DEAD HIGH-PILED
FOR LONG THIS DATE REMAINS IN THE MIND
OF THOSE THAT ON EARTH REMAIN BEHIND.

(40)

ON THE SUN IS SEEN WITH NAKED EYE
THE LARGEST BLACK STAIN
OSIRIS DESCENDS FROM HIS CHARIOT
ISIS RISES, MUCH MORE TRUE.

(41)

MARBLE MELTS IN THE HEAT
AND IN THE COLD LIKE WAX
THE HEAD SLIDES FROM THE FIRM BODY
CONTINUES IN THE DARK OF THE NIGHT.

(42)

THE SWEET WATER IS POISONED
IN ONE DAY THE DEAD OF A WAR
FOR LONG THIS DATE IN THE MINDS
OF THOSE REMAINING ON EARTH.

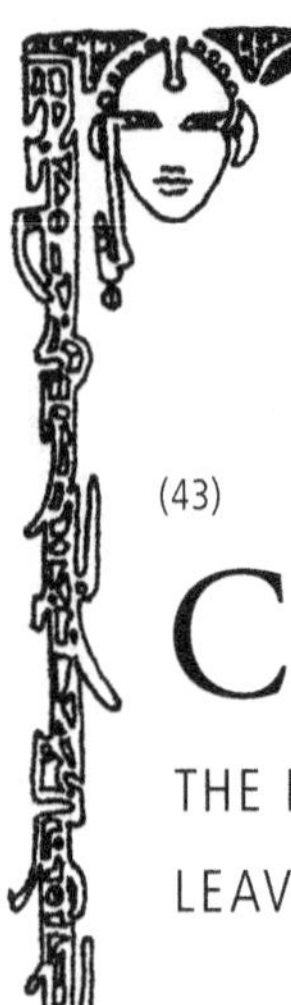

(43)

CATS AND DOGS COMMIT SUICIDE
UNDER THE FEW CARS AROUND THE TOWN
THE HEADS OF THE PEOPLE IN COMMAND,
LEAVE THE ARMS AND THE BODY FALLS DOWN.

(44)

A MAN OF POWER IS ASSASSINATED
IN THAT FOREIGN BEL PAESE* TERMINATED
SHOT IN THREE PLACES, ONE ABOVE THE FACE
ONE BELOW AND ONE ABOVE THE HEART'S PLACE
WHAT IS TRUE SPIRIT IS NOW MADE PLAIN
CAUSING MUCH GRIEVING AND MUCH PAIN.

(45)

THE POWER OF THE LITTLE LORD PREVAILS
RISEN EQUALLY IN THE LANDS INSANE
ALAS CERTAIN BRINGER OF PAIN
AS THE WIND RETURNS TO BLOW UPON THE SAILS**.

* Italy – the Bel Paese as described by Dante
**Windmill sails (TN)

(43)

THE CATS AND DOGS COMMIT SUICIDE
UNDER THE FEW CARS ON THE STREET
THE HEADS, OF THE PEOPLES IN COMMAND,
LEAVE THE ARMS AND THE BODY FALLS.

(44)

A POWERFUL MAN IS KILLED
IN THE FOREIGN BEL PAESE*
THREE SHOTS, ONE ABOVE THE FACE
TWO, ONE UNDER AND ONE OVER THE HEART
NOW THE SPIRIT WHICH IS TRUE REVEALS ITSELF
THAT CREATES MUCH MOURNING AND PAIN.

(45)

THE POWER OF THE LITTLE LORD
IS RISEN EQUALLY IN THE INSANE COUNTRIES
ALAS SURE BRINGER OF PAIN
JUST AS THE WIND RETURNS TO BLOW ON THE BLADES.

* Italy – the Bel Paese as described by Dante

(46)

THE MYTH THEN IS OUR MODEL AND OUR MIGHT
AND THE DESPERATE SEARCH CALLS
THE LITTLE LORD IS DANGEROUS AND HIS SITE
AND IF HE IS ANGRY A CITY FALLS.

(47)

BUT OVER THE AIR IN OPEN SPACE
COMES THE REPLY TO THIS ANCIENT FORCE
HUMANKIND WILL BELIEVE IT'S DISCOVERED HOW
TO BANISH HUNGER AND SWEAT OF BROW.

(48)

WHEN THE DAMAGE WILL HAVE BECOME CLEAR
AND THE SLOW MIND FINALLY COMPREHENDED
REALIZING THAT TO REDUCE SPENDING
THE GREEN BALANCE, THE SEASONS, ALL HAVE ENDED.

(46)

OF FORCE AND EXAMPLE IS THE MYTH
AND THE DESPERATE SEARCH APPEALS
DANGEROUS IS THE LITTLE LORD AND THE SITE
AND IF HE BECOMES ANGRY HE WIPES OUT A CITY.

(47)

BUT OVER THE AIR IN THE OPEN SPACE
IS THE REPLY TO THIS ANCIENT FORCE
HUMANKIND WILL BELIEVE TO HAVE DISCOVERED
HOW TO SATISFY HUNGER AND ELIMINATE TOIL.

(48)

WHEN THE DAMAGE WILL THEN BE EVIDENT
AND THE SLOW MIND WILL HAVE UNDERSTOOD
IT WILL REALIZE THAT TO REDUCE COSTS
THE BALANCE, THE GREEN, THE SEASONS WILL HAVE FINISHED.

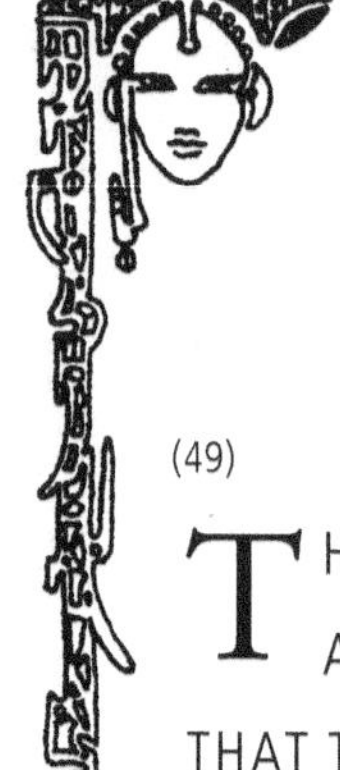

(49)

THE CLOCK HAS STOPPED IN THE PICTURE
AND THE LAST PAINTER HAS FOUND OUT
THAT THE GRASS'S COLOUR IS A MIXTURE
OF VIOLET AND OF RED, WITHOUT A DOUBT.

(50)

WHO SHALL PAINT THE PIT IN GREEN
AND THE TRUE TRACT WITH NEW BLOOD
THAT GUSHING FROM THE EARTH NO MORE IS SEEN
IF THE COURAGE THAT ONCE WAS, NO MORE I FIND?

(51)

THE COLOURS OF THE WATER ARE CHANGED QUITE
THE COLOURS IN THE HEAVENS WITHOUT NIGHT
ALL WHO SLEEP FROM SLEEP ARE TORN
IN THE AIR THE GRIM ROAR OF THE CAVES IS BORN.

(49)

FROM THE PICTURE THE CLOCK HAS STOPPED
AND THE FINAL PAINTER, DISCOVERED
HOW THE COLOURS OF THE GRASS MEADOW
ARE OF VIOLET AND RED MIXED IT IS CERTAIN.

(50)

WHO WILL PAINT THE PIT IN GREEN
AND THE TRUE PATH IN NEW BLOOD
THAT GUSHES FROM THE EARTH AND THEN IS LOST
IF I NO LONGER FIND COURAGE IN THOSE WHO HAD IT?

(51)

THE COLOURS OF THE WATER ARE CHANGED
THE COLOURS IN THE SKY WITHOUT NIGHT
ALL FROM SLEEP ARE TORN
IN THE AIR THE BLEAK ROAR OF THE CAVES.

(52)

THE REMEDY KILLS MANY MORE
THAN THE ILL IT SETS OUT TO CURE
THERE ARE NEW LAWS TO REVERSE THE HARM
BUT THE HEALTHY ARE EVER FEWER.

(53)

THAT WHICH WAS ONLY A CHILL
BECOMES PESTILENTIAL, A HORRID ILL
PEOPLE ARE HEALTHY, THEN WHY DO THEY DIE
THE PUBLIC HEALTH DOCTORS (HAVE PATIENCE) CRY.

(54)

AT SEA, NEVER-ENDING STORM WINDS BLOW
BRINGING SUFFERING AND DISTRESS
AND NOW ALL THIS YOU'VE COME TO KNOW
HOW TO AVOID THE HARM AND THE S.O.S?

(52)

THE REMEDY KILLS MANY MORE HUMANS
THAN THE ILLNESS IT WAS INTENDED TO CURE
NEW LAWS TO MODIFY THE DAMAGE
BUT FROM THE USE MADE FEW WILL BE HEALTHY.

(53)

THAT WHICH WAS ONLY A COLD
BECOMES GRIEF AND PESTILENCE
PEOPLE ARE HEALTHY, BUT WHY DO THEY DIE
CRIES THE STATE DOCTOR, HAVE PATIENCE.

(54)

ON THE SEA A NEVER ENDING STORM
DISPENSES TORMENT AND DISTRESS
AND NOW THAT YOU KNOW ALL THIS
HOW TO AVOID THE DAMAGE AND THE DANGER?

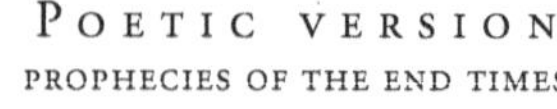

(55)

ROM THE SKY TWO TRAINS FELL
IN TWO COUNTRIES THE SAME DAY
IN THE FIRST NO ONE LIVED TO TELL
FEW (ALIVE) HANGING FROM THE SECOND TRAIN.

(56)

ETWEEN POLITICS AND BOMBS THERE'S NO ACCORD
BUT A NEW HOT BED OF TERROR
ARRIVES WHEN THE PRISONERS OF THE FJORD
ARE STRICKEN BY THE AVIATOR.

(57)

EW BLACK MUD IS WELLING
WHERE IT WAS NOT EXPECTED
NEW FORGES ARE BUSY MILLING
WHEN HOPE HAD DEFECTED.

(55)

FROM THE SKY TWO TRAINS FELL
THE SAME DAY IN TWO COUNTRIES
OF THE FIRST ALL THE TRAVELLERS SILENCED
A FEW OF THE SECOND (ALIVE) HUNG ON.

(56)

POLITICS AND BOMBS DO NOT GET ALONG
BUT A NEW HOT BED OF TERROR
ARRIVES WHEN THE PRISONERS OF THE FJORD
ARE HIT BY THE AVIATOR.

(57)

NEW BLACK MUD RISES
WHERE IT WAS NOT LOOKED FOR
NEW FORGES WHIRL AT WORK
WHEN HOPE WAS FADING.

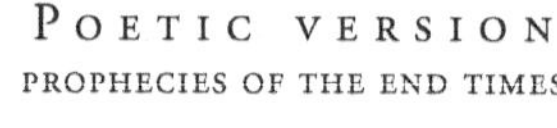

(58)

THE NEW ALLIANCES VIEWED WITH SUSPICION
WITH PAPER AND PICTURES THE PEOPLE DRIVEN
SHEEP, DOGS AND DEER ARE THE IMPRESSION
THE WHITE TERRITORY OF OVERSEAS
BURNT AND BROKEN WITH THE PALISADE
HE WHO'S GREAT IS READY, STAYS AND SEES.

(59)

MANY ARE THE SUICIDES AND LIFE
IS VOID, ITS PURPOSE ALL DIMINISHED,
OR, NOT KNOWING WHAT TO DO YOU LAUGH
THE AGE IS CLOSED AND IT IS FINISHED.

(60)

ALSO FROM A FAR OFF LAND
WITH A NUMBER YOU SPEAK AND SEE
THE EMBLEM RIGHTS ITSELF WITH THE HAND
YOU NOD YOUR HEAD YET DON'T BELIEVE.

(58)

THE NEW ALLIANCES REGARDED WITH SUSPICION
WITH PAPER AND IMAGES THE PEOPLE ARE DIRECTED
SHEEP, DOGS AND FALLOW DEER THE EFFECT MUST BE
THE WHITE TERRITORY OF BEYOND THE SEA
BURNT AND BROKEN WITH THE PALISADE
WHOEVER IS BIG IS READY AND STAYS TO WATCH.

(59)

MANY ARE THE SUICIDES
AND PURPOSES IN LIFE ARE LOST
OR IF YOU DON'T KNOW WHAT TO DO YOU LAUGH
THE ERA IS CLOSED AND IS FINISHED.

(60)

EVEN FROM VERY FAR AWAY
WITH A NUMBER YOU SPEAK AND SEE
THE INSIGNIA IS STRAIGHTENED WITH THE HAND
YOU NOD YOUR HEAD AND YET DON'T BELIEVE.

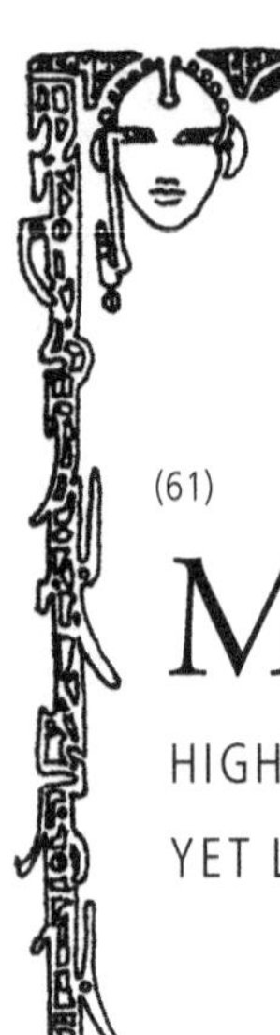

(61)

MANY BANNERS, SECRET SOCIETIES
YET HEARTS MADE OF VIOLENCE AND EMPTINESS
HIGH AND SUBLIME ARE THEIR DECLARED AIMS
YET LIVES WITH SCARCITY THEY OPPRESS.

(62)

INHALING AND DRINKING HIDE THE TRUTHS
FROM WHICH THE NEW MAN REELS BACK
YOU TOOK INSUFFICIENT CARE, O YOUTHS
AND THE COURAGE, STRENGTH, NOW I SEE THEM LACK.

(63)

OUR CHILDREN ALL ARE TEMPTED
RAISED WITH FEED LIKE CHICKENS
THE PARENTS WILL REALIZE THEY HAVE RAISED
A HUMANITY THAT MENTALLY SICKENS.

(61)

MANY ENSIGNS, SECRET COMPANIES
BUT EMPTY AND VIOLENT ARE THE HEARTS
HIGH AND SUBLIME DECLARED AIMS
SUPPRESSING LIVES THROUGH HARDSHIP.

(62)

INHALING AND DRINKING ARE HIDDEN
TRUTHS FROM WHICH THE NEW MAN FLEES,
YOUTH, YOU WERE NOT CAREFUL ENOUGH
AND NOW THE COURAGE, THE STRENGTH I NO LONGER FIND.

(63)

THE CHILDREN ARE TEMPTED
RAISED WITH FEED LIKE CHICKENS
THE FATHERS, WRETCHED, WILL REALISE
THEY HAVE RAISED A HUMANITY OF MADMEN.

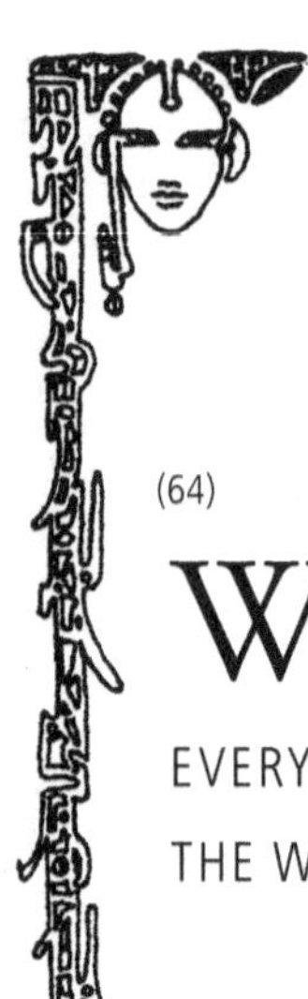

(64)

WITHOUT PREPARATION FOR HARD GRIND
PEOPLE INCREASINGLY LOSE THEIR MIND
EVERYTHING HAPPENS IN A MOMENT
THE WORLD WANTS CLEANSING FOR IT IS SPENT.

(65)

WHEN THE SAME WORDS
FROM THE SAME MOUTHS ARE REPORTED
THIS WILL SIGNAL THE OFFSPRING ARE DEGENERATE
SAME BRAINS, WITHOUT THOUGHT AND MINDS DISTORTED.

(66)

MANKIND REALISES, WHILE IN CRISIS PROFOUND,
THE ABSURDITY OF MONEY AND THE CONSUMERITE
CHANGING THE HEAD, RISKS AND GOOD ROUNDS
WHILE THE MANSIONS OF PAPER ARE ALL ALIGHT.

(64)

WITHOUT TRAINING TO TOIL
COMFORTABLY ARISES THE MADNESS
EVERYTHING HAPPENS QUICKER DONE THAN SAID
THE WORLD IS TIRED AND WANTS CLEANSING.

(65)

WHEN THE SAME WORDS
ARE REPEATED FROM THE SAME MOUTHS
IT WILL BE A SIGN THAT PROGENY ARE DEGENERATE
SAME BRAINS, WITHOUT THOUGHT AND CRAZY MINDS.

(66)

MANKIND REALISES, IN DEEP CRISIS,
ABOUT ABSURD MONEY AND CONSUMERISM
CHANGE THE HEAD, RISKS AND KEEP GOOD WATCH
WHILE THE MANSIONS OF PAPER ARE UP IN SMOKE.

(67)

FALLS A CITY
TAKEN AND ANNIHILATED
DEATH DESCENDS UPON EVERY AGE
AFRICA SHAKES AND IS DEVASTATED.

(68)

OF ASIA OF EUROPE, THE MOUNTAIN FIRE
THE AMERICAS SEPARATED
HIGHWAYS RUINED, THE BRIDGES ALL BROKEN UP
THE RAILWAYS DEVASTATED.

(69)

EXHAUSTED IS THE INNER SEA
AND THE FOREST BLEEDING
THE LATE ALARM LED BY THE FRANK
MOVES SLOWLY, AND NO ONE HEEDING.

(67)

A CITY FALLS
TAKEN AND DESTROYED
DEATH DESCENDS UPON EVERY AGE
AFRICA SHAKES AND IS DEVASTATED.

(68)

THE FIRE OF THE MOUNTAINS IN ASIA, IN EUROPE,
THE AMERICAS SEPARATED
THE STREETS RUINED, THE BRIDGES BROKEN UP
THE RAILWAYS DAMAGED.

(69)

THE INNER SEA IS TIRED
THE FOREST BLOODLESS
THE FRANK LEADS THE LATE ALARM
MOVES SLOWLY, AND IS NOT LISTENED TO.

(70)

ONE MAN, ONE FAMILY
FROM THE HOLY EMPIRE IS RAISED
BEHIND AN IRON GRILL ACTS SWIFTLY
BUT LIKE CHARLEMAGNE BY SQUIRE BETRAYED.

(71)

THE STRONG MAN IT TOOK SO LONG TO FIND
HAS A SYMBOL BETWEEN THE SEA AND MOUNTAIN
AND AS POLYPHEMUS WAS MADE BLIND
OVER THE NEW EMPIRE A NEW FOUNTAIN.

(72)

SEE A NEW FRONT UPON EUROPE LOOM
ALTERING LIKE A SERPENT SINUOUSLY
FROM ROME BY DAY WITH A BROOM
AT EVENING THE CHANGE, UP IN TURIN CITY.

(70)

A MAN, ONE FAMILY
ARISES FROM THE HOLY EMPIRE
ACTS QUICK BEHIND AN IRON GRILL
BUT LIKE CHARLEMAGNE, THE SQUIRE BETRAYS.

(71)

THE STRONG MAN SEARCHED FOR FOR SO LONG
HAS A CREST BETWEEN SEA AND MOUNTAIN
AND AS POLYPHEMUS WAS BLINDED
FOR THE NEW EMPIRE A NEW SOURCE.

(72)

A NEW FRONT IN EUROPE
CHANGES LIKE A SERPENT MOVING
BY DAY GOES FROM ROME BY BROOMSTICK
IN THE EVENING THE CHANGE, UP IN TURIN.

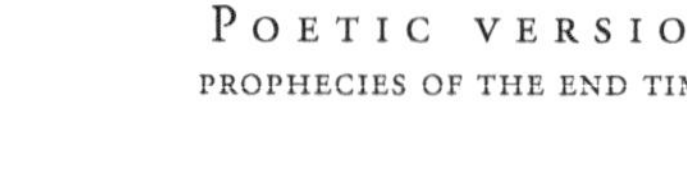

(73)

MILAN IS CELEBRATING
THE SNOW IN ABUNDANCE FALLING
FALSE AMAZEMENT, LAUGHTER IN THE HEAD.
SUDDENLY THE AIR IS ALIGHT AND THE PARADE IS DEAD.

(74)

ALSO THE CELEBRATED ASTROLOGER FORETOLD
AND BEFORE THAT THE EGYPTIAN OLD
FROM THE SEA OF HEAVENS A SMOKY DAY
THE GREAT CONFLICT FALLS UPON ITS PREY.

(75)

THE EAGLE AND THE LION UNITED
AS ONCE THEY WERE DIVIDED
QUARRELS THEY WILL PICK TO TIP THE SCALES
BETWEEN LONG KNIVES AND MANY SMILES.

(73)

MILAN IS CELEBRATING;
THE SNOW FELL IN ABUNDANCE
FALSE AMAZEMENT, LAUGHTER IN THE HEAD
SUDDENLY THE AIR IS ALIGHT AND THE PARADE DIES.

(74)

ALSO THE FAMOUS ASTROLOGER
SPOKE OF IT AND THE EGYPTIAN EVEN BEFORE
FROM THE SEA OF SKY A SMOKY DAY
THE GREAT CONFLICT DESCENDS AND STRIKES.

(75)

THE EAGLE AND THE LION UNITED
AS ONCE THEY WERE DIVIDED
TO TIP THE BALANCE THEY WILL FOMENT QUARRELS
BETWEEN LONG KNIVES AND MANY SMILES.

(76)

THE BEAR HAS TWO NESTS
ONE IN A FAR OFF ICY LAND
THE OTHER BY THE AFRICAN BEACHES
BE WARY WHEN IT OFFERS YOU A HAND.

(77)

THAT WELL RENOWNED CLOCK
TO NO AVAIL STOPPED
DURING THE HOUR OF RESPITE
ARMED WAS THE HAND FOR FIGHT.

(78)

SONGS AND THE NEW FASHION
WHILE THE SACK IS COMPRESSED
CITIES LIKE BABEL ENJOY WITH PASSION
THE LAST NIGHT, FIRST NIGHT OF THE REST.

(76)

THE BEAR HAS TWO NESTS
ONE ON THE ICE FAR AWAY
THE OTHER NEAR THE AFRICAN SHORES
BE CAREFUL WHEN IT OFFERS YOU A HAND.

(77)

THE FAMOUS CLOCK
STOPPED IN VAIN
DURING THE HOUR OF REST
ARMED WAS THE HAND.

(78)

SONGS AND NEW FASHION
WHILE THE BAG IS SQUEEZED
A CITY LIKE BABEL ENJOYS
THE LAST NIGHT AND FIRST OF THE FIRST.

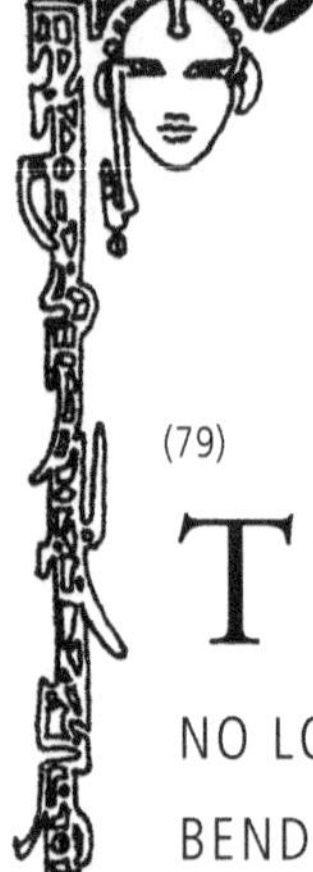

(79)

THE SUCCESSOR TO PETER
REVERTS TO THE NAME OF YORE
NO LONGER IS ABLE TO LEAVE THE GLASS
BENDING HIS BACK TO MANY BURDENS MORE.

(80)

FULL OF RICHES IS THE GREAT CHURCH
THE LAST KING AND THE LAST LIFE EXPEDITED
HE TOO SHALL HAVE TO BEND HIS BACK
SINCE ONLY FOOLS SEE IT STILL UNITED.

(81)

HALF THE BELLS TOLL A MOURNING KNELL
HALF RING OUT FOR HURRIED FEASTING
THE THRONE DESTROYED WHERE IT FELL
THE FIRE AROUND THE CROSSES LICKING.

(79)

THE SUCCESSOR OF PETER
HAS RETAKEN THE OLD NAME
HE WILL NO LONGER BE ABLE TO LEAVE THE GLASS
BUT WILL BEND THE BACK TO MANY BURDENS.

(80)

THE GREAT CHURCH FULL OF RICHES
THE LAST KING AND THE LAST LIFE
HE TOO WILL HAVE TO BEND HIS BACK
BECAUSE IT IS FOLLY TO SEE IT STILL UNITED.

(81)

HALF THE BELLS RING IN MOURNING
HALF FOR QUICK CELEBRATIONS
THE THRONE FALLS AND IS DESTROYED
THE FIRE WINDS AROUND THE CROSSES.

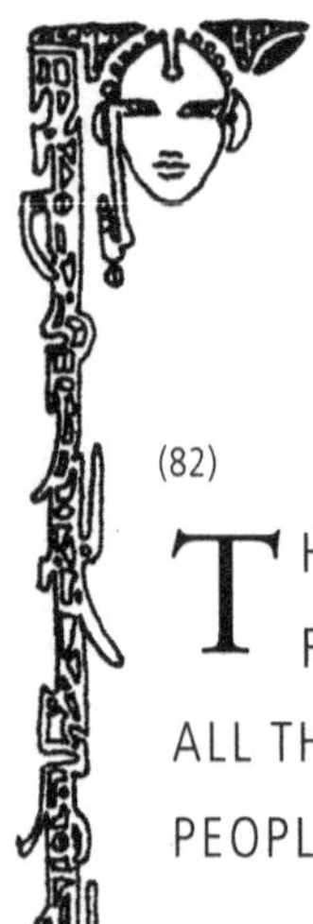

(82)

THE BELL THAT NO ONE SOUNDS
FALLS ROLLING FROM THE TOWER
ALL THE CITY RESOUNDS
PEOPLE SCREAM IN MADNESS REELING.

(83)

ICE AND SNOW DESCEND ON THE PALMS
ALSO THE RED-HOT DESERTS ADVANCE
THINGS NEVER SEEN, DEATH TAKES
THE WIND WHIRLS IN ITS DANCE.

(84)

ALPS AND PYRAMIDS ALIKE IN THE BITTER COLD
ICEBERGS BREAK UP AND WANDER AS NEVER OF OLD
FAST CLOUDS RACE ACROSS THE SKIES
RUMBLES, RIVERS, AND GIANTS' CRIES.

(82)

THE BELL THAT NOBODY RINGS
DESCENDS FROM THE TOWER ROLLING
ALL THE CITY RESOUNDS
THE PEOPLE GO MAD SCREAMING.

(83)

ICE AND SNOW DESCEND ON THE PALMS
ALSO THE RED-HOT DESERT ADVANCES
THINGS NEVER SEEN, DEATH CLAIMS
THE WIND WHIRLS IN ITS DANCE.

(84)

ALPS AND PYRAMIDS SIMILAR IN THE BITTER COLD
THE ICE BREAKS UP AND WANDERS AS NEVER BEFORE
FAST CLOUDS RACE IN THE SKY
RUMBLES, RIVERS, CRIES OF GIANTS.

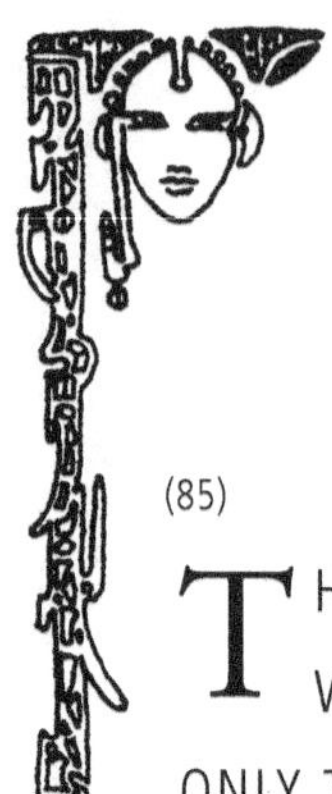

(85)

THE READY FEW FIGHT EACH OTHER INTERNECINE
WHILE THE COMMON ENEMY STAYS TO GLOAT
ONLY THE CITY WITH THE BULL ITS ENSIGN
HAS FEW CHILDREN KNOWING HOW TO HOPE.

(86)

THE ASTROLOGER RETURNS AT OUR CALLING
THE PEOPLE SEARCH IN MIGHTY DREAD
THOUSANDS QUESTION THE FATE BEFALLING
IN ANSWERS EVER THE SAME (IS) THE SEED.

(87)

THE MOUNTAIN SLIDES IN THE LAKE
AND THE WATER PRESSES AGAINST THE GREAT DAM WALL
ALL THAT REMAINS IS A MEMORY VAGUE
FOR MANY YEARS THE EAR RIPENS NOT ALL.

(85)

THE READY FEW FIGHT AMONGST EACH OTHER
WHILE THE COMMON ENEMY IS WATCHING
THE LONE CITY WITH THE SYMBOL OF THE BULL*
HAS FEW CHILDREN WHO WILL BE ABLE TO HOPE.

(86)

THE ASTROLOGER RETURNS WHEN HE IS CALLED
THE PEOPLE SEARCH AND FEAR
THOUSANDS AND THOUSANDS QUESTIONING THE FATE
IN THE REPLIES, ALWAYS THE SAME, (IS) THE SEED.

(87)

THE MOUNTAIN SLIDES IN THE LAKE
AND THE WATER PRESSES AGAINST THE GREAT DAM
ALL THAT REMAINS IS A VAGUE MEMORY
FOR MANY YEARS THE EAR NO LONGER RIPENS.

* Turin

(88)

THE OLD ORDER, AND THE HEADS OF IT
ON THE EARTH HAVE LEFT THEIR BONES
MALADROIT THE NEW WILL SURELY FALL
ENDING SOON IN THE SAME PIT.

(89)

THE SOCIETIES FALSELY CHANGED TOO FAST
STRIKES AFFECTION PAINS AND CRIMES
THOSE TIRED OF DUTIES THEIR TOOLS ASIDE WOULD CAST
CREATE FOR ONE AND ALL HARD TIMES.

(90)

SCANDALS OF MEN IN POWER ARE PLAIN
THOUGH FALSELY COVERED UP
EVERYONE KNOWS THEY MUST REFRAIN
FROM SPEAKING OUT AND TAKE THEIR CUT.

(88)

ALL THE HEADS OF THE OLD POWER
ON THE EARTH HAVE LEFT THEIR BONES
THE NEW CLUMSY WILL HAVE TO FALL
ENDING SOON IN THE SAME PIT.

(89)

THE SOCIETIES FALSELY CHANGED IN HASTE
STRIKES ROBBERIES PAIN AFFECTIONS
WHO TIRES OF DUTY THROWS AWAY THE TOOL
CREATES HARD TIMES AGAIN FOR ALL.

(90)

SCANDALS OF MEN IN POWER
ARE PLAIN, FALSELY HIDDEN
SO THAT EVERYONE KNOWS THEIR DUTY
REPRESS AND POCKET THE PAYOFF.

(91)

WINGS ON FIELD LIKE CROSSED SWORDS CLASH
ROLLING BIRDS OF FIRE
BURN FLESH AND METAL IN A FLASH
OF FOUR HUNDRED FEW ARE LEFT ALIVE.

(92)

TALKING OF OUR FRIENDS WITH SMILING MIEN
SINCERE IN HOUR OF NEED AND TRIAL
MANY MANY WILL THEM DEMEAN
THE GOOD RECEIVED IN FRANK DENIAL.

(93)

TRIALS AND SIGNS OF THE TIMES, PERFIDIOUS
FLATTERY OF FRIENDS FALSELY TREACHEROUS
THESE EVIL WORDS WILL EVER CIRCULATE
AND EACH REPETITION WILL THE ILL INFLATE.

(91)

WINGS AS CROSSED SWORDS ON THE FIELD
ROLLING BIRDS OF FIRE
BURN FLESH AND METAL IN A FLASH
OF FOUR HUNDRED THOSE THAT LIVE ARE FEW.

(92)

OF MEN AND WOMEN FRIENDS, WITH SMILING FACES
SINCERE IN NEED AND IN HELP
THEY WILL SPEAK EVIL AND TO MANY MANY PEOPLE
HIDING THE GOOD RECEIVED.

(93)

SIGNS AND TRIALS OF THE TIMES ARE
THE FLATTERY OF TRAITOROUS FALSE FRIENDS
THE EVIL WORD WILL GO WANDERING
REPEATED INFLATED IN ALL GATHERINGS.

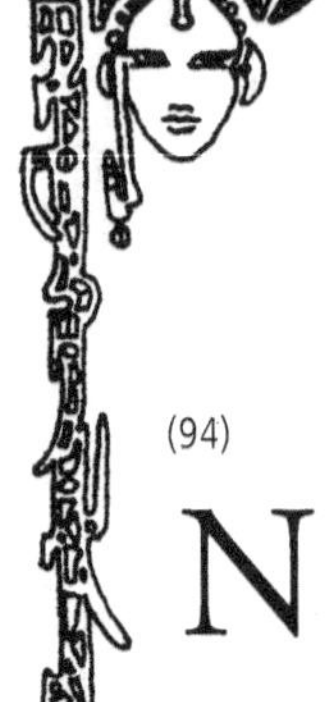

(94)

NOW TIMES ARE OF FOLLY BLIND
AND THE FRIEND FOR LOVE IS SLAIN
EVERY GOOD WORK FORGOTTEN BY THE MIND
SEEN DISTORTED, ONE ACTS WITH FURY'S BANE.

(95)

NEW ANIMAL AND INSECT NEW
ODDLY STRANGE, YET PART OF LIFE
IN THE SEA CAN SEEM TO BE ASKEW
COUNT THE STRANGE ON FINGERS FOUR.

(96)

LIGHTNING AND RAIN—HAIL—WEAPONS HAVE BECOME
AND THREATENING TO PEOPLE ON THE LAND
I AM SEER OF THIS AND SEE IN HORROR NUMB
HORRENDOUS WINDS AND FEW DAYS OF CALM.

(94)

NOW TIMES ARE OF FOLLY
THE FRIEND MURDERED FOR LOVE
EVERY GOOD WORK THE MIND FORGETS
SEES DISTORTED, ACTS WITH FURY.

(95)

NEW ANIMAL AND NEW INSECT
STRANGE, BUT PART OF LIFE
IN THE SEA CAN APPEAR INEPT
THE STRANGE MUST COUNT ON FOUR FINGERS.

(96)

LIGHTNING AND RAIN—HAIL—IN WEAPONS TRANSFORMED
ARE THREATS TO PEOPLE ON THE LAND
I AM A SEER OF WHAT I SEE IN HORROR
HORRENDOUS WINDS AND FEW CALM DAYS.

(97)

THE NEW IS NO LONGER NEW
DEATH STALKS AND PRISONERS BREAK OUT
SCARCE WORK NOW I CANNOT FIND
VIOLENCE AND MADNESS ALL ABOUT.

(98)

NEW ILLNESSES INVENTED
BY PHYSICIANS QUITE DEMENTED
ARMS AND LEGS UNDERGO AMPUTATION
RUSH, HOSPITAL, MONEY AND LITIGATION.

(99)

MADNESS RENDERS THOSE CONTENTED
WHO STILL HEALTHY ARE DISMEMBERED
BECAUSE THIS WAS CARRIED OUT WITH SKILL
AND THE UNFORTUNATE ARE LIVING STILL.

(97)

T HE NEW IS NO LONGER NEW
DEAD AND ESCAPES FROM THE PRISONS
SCARCE WORK I NO LONGER FIND
VIOLENCE AND MADNESS MARCH IN LEGIONS.

(98)

N EW ILLNESSES INVENTED
BY PHYSICIANS GONE MAD
ARMS AND LEGS ARE CUT OFF
RUSHING, HOSPITAL, MONEY AND LITIGATION.

(99)

M ADNESS MAKES THOSE HAPPY
WHO WERE DISMEMBERED WHILE STILL HEALTHY
BECAUSE THIS WAS DONE WITH SKILL
AND THE UNFORTUNATES ARE STILL ALIVE.

(100)

EVERY PART OF THE BODY RUNS WILD
THIS IS THE HORRENDOUS TRENDY MALADY
WITH FALSE CURED TUMOURS LIFE WILL BE
TORN ASUNDER AND THE SOUL SET FREE.

(101)

SNOW AND WIND DESCEND IN METRES
AND THE RICH DISTRICTS FROZE
RANGING ABROAD FURY AND BLACK SPECTRES
PRECIOUS SHIPS FROM THE RIVER ROSE.

(102)

MILLENIUM CURRENTS OF ICE AND SEA
FROM THEIR PATHS NOW DEVIATE
IN WARM SEAS THEY TRAVEL SOLEMNLY
DANGEROUS ANYWHERE SHIPS MAY BE.

(100)

EVERY PART OF THE BODY GONE MAD
HORRENDOUS IS THE TRENDY ILLNESS
WITH A FALSE TUMOR CURED LIFE WILL BE
TORN AND THE SOUL RETURNED.

(101)

SNOW AND WIND DESCEND IN METRES
AND THE RICH DISTRICTS FROZE
FURY AND BLACK SPECTRES WANDER
THE RIVER HAS RAISED UP PRECIOUS SHIPS.

(102)

ICE AND CURRENTS OF MILLENNIA
DEVIATED FROM THEIR PATH
IN WARM SEAS SOLEMNLY THEY TRAVEL
DANGEROUS ANYWHERE SHIPS GO.

(103)

THE FISHING WAR FROM FIRE WROUGHT
THE BATTLE ON THE SEAS IS NOW FULL FOLD
THE FISHING INCREASES, AND FEW ARE CAUGHT
THE BLOOD REDDENS, THE SIREN COMES, BEHOLD.

(104)

THE SLAUGHTER NOW IS MADE OF MAN
WITH PIKES, NETS, SHOTS AND ACCIDENT
IN THE SEA STRAIT THE DANCE BEGAN
LOOKING WITH SUSPICION AT THE ORIENT.

(105)

SKY AND SEA BY FLEETS ARE OVERRUN
THREATS OF INVASION FROM DISTANT LANDS
"BRING THEM TO THEIR KNEES" BESEECHES EVERYONE
THE WELLS MINED, PILES OF MONEY IN THEIR HANDS.

(103)

THE FISH WAR BECOMES FIERY
THE BATTLE ON THE SEAS IS ALL AROUND
THE FISHING INCREASES, FEW ARE THE FISH
THE BLOOD REDENS AND THE SIREN COMES.

(104)

THE SLAUGHTER NOW OF MEN IS MADE
WITH PIKES, NETS AND SHOTS, THE INCIDENT
ON THE NARROW SEA BEGAN THE DANCE
THE ORIENT IS LOOKED AT WITH SUSPICION.

(105)

SKY AND SEA FULL OF FLEETS
THREATS OF INVASION FROM DISTANT LANDS
UNANIMOUSLY "WE WILL BRING THEM TO THEIR KNEES"
THE MINED WELLS, MONEY IN HANDFULS.

(106)

IN WOMEN THE CYCLE IS ALL UNDONE
ABORTIONS, THICK BLOOD AND CRYING
MADNESS AND SUICIDE UNDER AN IRATE SUN
SADNESS AND O'ER THE MIND A MANTLE LYING.

(107)

THE ATOM'S NEW SECRETS NOW UNFOLD
NEW RAYS PROJECTING HEAT AND COLD
MEN AND THUNDER IN FLIGHT WEAVE THEIR NET
FIRE MONSTERS IN THE SKY THAT LINGER YET.

(108)

OF GREAT POWER IS THE METAL NEW
STRANGE ITS USE, LIGHTS VARIOUS ILLUMINATE
THE VOICES OF THE YELLOW FOLK ARE TRUE
THE STRANGER ASKS, REQUESTS TO FORMULATE.

(106)

IN WOMEN THE CYCLE IS CHANGED
ABORTIONS, FAT BLOOD AND WEEPING
MADNESS SUICIDE UNDER THE IRATE SUN
SADNESS AND A MANTLE ON THE MIND.

(107)

THE ATOM REVEALS NEW SECRETS
NEW RAYS FOR HEAT AND COLD
MEN AND THUNDER IN FLIGHT WEAVE NETS
MONSTERS OF FIRE REMAIN IN THE SKY.

(108)

NEW METAL OF GREAT POWER
STRANGE USE AND DIFFERENT LIGHTS
OF THE YELLOW PEOPLE THE VOICES ARE TRUE
THE FOREIGNER ASKS, THE REQUESTS HAVING EMERGED.

(109)

PRIESTS OF THESE, THE LATTER DAYS
YET PRIESTS THEY ARE OF DREAD
FEAR AND TERROR, THE WICKED PRAYS
FEW THE TRUE WINGS ON THE WIND OUTSPREAD.

(110)

AIR FROM OUT THE EARTH DOES SPIRE
BURNS AND CONSUMES ITSELF ENTIRE
THE ICE DRIVES OUT THE HEAT AS IN HOT HOUSES
THE WARMTH SUBSIDES, THE CHIMNEY SMOKE RISES.

(111)

FIREWOOD THEN IS SOUGHT AND IS NOT FOUND
MONEY, MONEY, FOR EVERYTHING A PRICE
THE ROMAN HIDES IT IN THE GROUND
SOME DIE, SOME REST, AS DESCENDS THE ICE.

(109)

PRIESTS IN THE END TIMES
BUT PRIESTS OF FRIGHT
FEAR AND TERROR, THE PRAYERS OF THE WICKED
FEW THE TRUE WINGS SPREAD ON THE WIND.

(110)

THE AIR THAT ISSUES FROM THE EARTH
BURNS AND CONSUMES ITSELF
THE BITTER COLD BANISHES HEAT AS IN GREENHOUSES
THE WARMTH CEASES AND THE CHIMNEY SMOKES.

(111)

THE SEARCH FOR WOOD IS THEN IN VAIN
MONEY, MONEY FOR EVERYTHING
SO THE ROMAN HIDES IT IN THE LAIR
THE COLD DESCENDS, SOME DIE AND SOME REST.

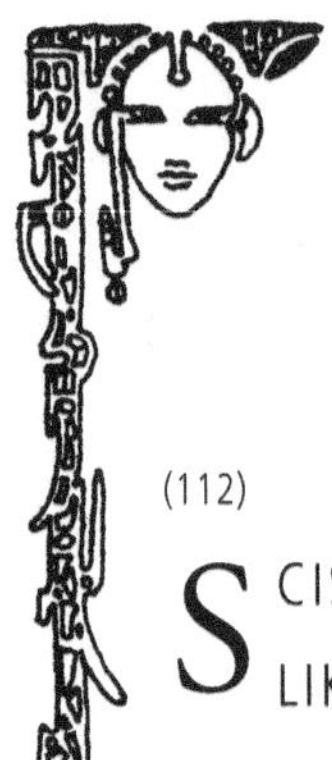

(112)

SCISSORS HAVE CUT THE STRING
LIKE THE SHOE IN THE GATHERING
SEEKING ASYLUM THE RULERS COME
O SPIRIT OF THE TWO LORDS STRONG BECOME.

(113)

JUST AS THE SIRENS SONG
ENCHANTED THE SALT SEA RUNNERS
FLEETS SEARCHING FOR THE FISH SO LONG
END UP IN CONFLICT AND IN HORRORS.

(114)

THE LITTLE LORD IS MELTED FROM THE SKY
LIGHTNING HIGHER THAN THE CLOUDS ARE HIGH
THE TOWERS OF IRON CARRIERS OF AGONY
TRANSFORMED LIKE WOLVES INTO DOGS BY ALCHEMY.

(112)

SCISSORS HAVE CUT THE THREAD
LIKE THE SHOE IN THE ASSEMBLY
SOVEREIGNS OF COUNTRIES WILL SEEK REFUGE
THE SPIRIT OF THE TWO LORDS MUST SHOW.

(113)

JUST AS THE SONG OF THE SIRENS
ENCHANTING THE SAILORS OF THE SEAS
THE FLEET SEARCHING LONG FOR THE FISH
CROSSES INTO THE FIGHT AND INTO THE HORROR.

(114)

FROM THE SKY IS UNLEASHED THE LITTLE LORD
LIGHTNING BOLTS HIGHER THAN THE CLOUDS
THE TOWERS OF IRON CARRIERS OF PAIN
BY ALCHEMY WERE CHANGED AS WOLVES INTO DOGS.

(115)

NEW CURRENTS BY POWER DECIDED
HEATING THE FROZEN SEAS
FIVE NATIONS OBSERVING SEATED
FIGHTING WITH MUTILATED INFANTRIES.

(116)

THE DELAY HAS POISONED THE SEAS
WHERE MADNESS AND FURY DANCED AT EASE
A LEADEN MASK FROM THE HEAVENS SEEMS TO FALL
AND WITH IT LIFE IS CANCELLED ALL.

(117)

FIRE AND SMOKE INDUCED INTO THE WOODS
WHERE LIFE SUFFOCATES AND DIES WITHIN IT
THE DAMAGE IS TRULY GRAVE AS IT COULD,
FORGOTTEN OR FETED THE ONE WHO DID IT.

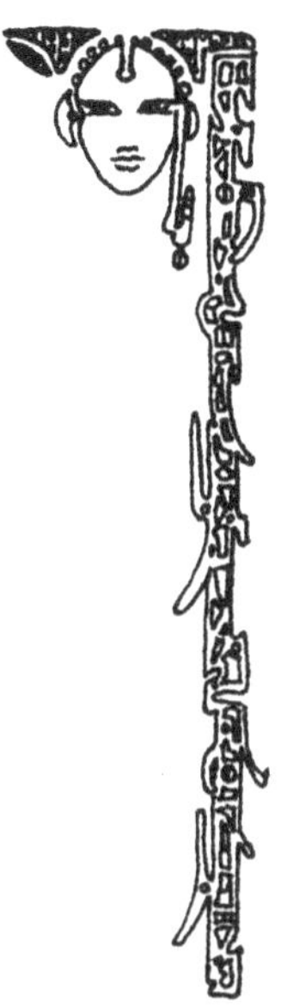

(115)

NEW CURRENTS BY POWER DECIDED
HEATING THE FROZEN SEAS
FIVE NATIONS OBSERVE SITTING DOWN
FIGHTING WITH MUTILATED INFANTRY.

(116)

THE DELAY HAS POISONED THE SEA
WHERE MADNESS AND FURY HAVE DANCED
A LEADEN MASK FROM THE SKY SEEMS TO
HAVE DESCENDED, AND LIFE CANCELLED.

(117)

FIRE AND SMOKE INDUCED IN THE FORESTS
WHERE LIFE IS SUFFOCATED AND DIES
THE DAMAGE IS TRULY GRAVE LIKE THE PLAGUE
FORGOTTEN OR PRAISED WAS THE INFECTOR.

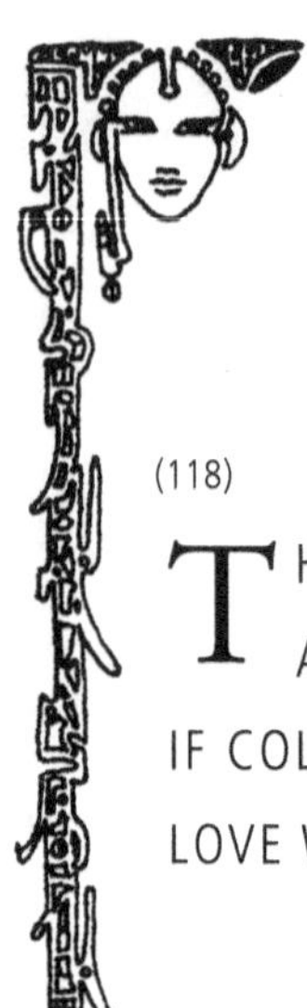

(118)

THE YOUNG CONTEMPTUOUS AND BASE OF MIND
AS LONG THAT IS, THAT THE HOME IS SNUG
IF COLD AND HUNGER UNDER THRESHOLD SLIDE
LOVE WILL EVAPORATE LIKE THAT OF DOG.

(119)

WOMEN ALIKE TO MEN WITH CRAZY MIND
[POLITICAL] PARTIES FIRE DECISIONS AND SO
THE LIKE-MINDED RARELY CAN I FIND
UPON THEIR THRONES THE NOBLES COME AND GO.

(120)

FLESH IS CUT AND THEN RESEWN
WHILE PAIN ENVELOPS THE WORLD'S WIDE BOUND
THE ABSURD WORK SEEMS TO SUCCEED
BUT WHAT IS SQUARE CANNOT BE ROUND.

(118)

THE YOUNG CONTEMPTUOUS AND BASE OF MIND
AS LONG AS THE HOME IS COMFORTABLE
IF COLD AND HUNGER UNDER THRESHOLD SLIDE
LOVE WILL EVAPORATE LIKE THAT OF DOG.

(119)

MADNESS OF WOMEN IS ALIKE TO MEN
[POLITICAL]PARTIES FIRE AND DECISIONS
THE LIKE-MINDED HAVE BECOME RARE
AND NOBLES COME AND GO ON THE THRONES.

(120)

FLESH CUT AND RESEWN
MEANWHILE PAIN ENVELOPS ALL THE WORLD
THE ABSURD WORK SEEMS TO HAVE SUCCEEDED
BUT THAT WHICH IS SQUARE DOES NOT BECOME ROUND.

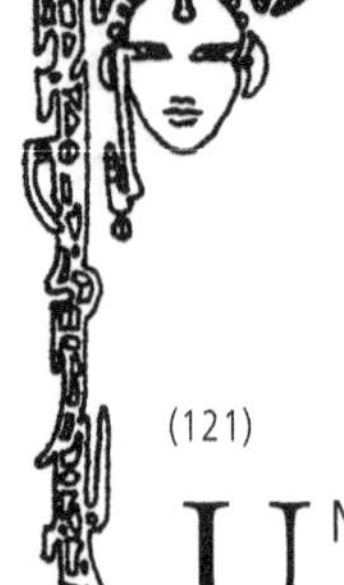

(121)

UNKNOWN HEAT WHERE THE ICE PERSPIRES
FLOODS OF SUMMER AND SUDDEN FIRES
THE SEVERE RISK IS TO BE SUFFOCATED
THE EARTH SHAKES WHERE RICE IS CULTIVATED.

(122)

BURNING MIRRORS RISE IN THE FIRMAMENT
AND THE SUN SHINES IN THE MIDNIGHT SKY
JUST AS THE SAILS OF ROMAN SHIPS WERE BURNT
TODAY IT WILL BURN THE FLEETS FROM ON HIGH.

(123)

IN THE SIXTH HOUR OF THE DAY
GREAT DESTRUCTION WILL HOLD SWAY
NOTHING REMAINING, THE PORTS UNDER WATER
THE WIND A TYRANT GIVES NO QUARTER.

(121)

UNKNOWN HEAT WHERE THE COLD IS SWEAT

FLOODS OF SUMMER AND SUDDEN FIRE

THE SEVERE RISK IS SUFFOCATING

THE EARTH TREMBLES WHERE RICE IS BORN.

(122)

BURNING MIRRORS HAVE RISEN INTO THE SKY

AND THE SUN SHINES AT MIDNIGHT

AS IT BURNT THE SAIL OF THE ROMANS SHIPS

TODAY, FROM ON HIGH, IT WILL BURN THE FLEETS.

(123)

IN THE SIXTH HOUR

THERE WILL BE GREAT DAMAGE

THE PORTS ARE SUBMERGED AND NOTHING REMAINS

THE WIND IS A GREAT TYRANT.

AFTERWORD

Falco Tarassaco wrote the *Prophecies* in November 1976 and they were published in some issues of the monthly *Notiziario Horus* (Horus Bulletin), in no particular order, starting from September 1977. About three years later, in 1980, the prophecies were collected together and published in the first edition of this book. Their one hundred and twenty-three quatrains are written in the same hermetic style of Nostradamus' Centuries, to which the title of this book makes explicit reference.

In order to comprehend the meaning of these quatrains it is necessary to use various types of logic, as there are many riddles and plays on words. The first question researchers ask themselves is: in which order did Falco write them? The order in which the first publications appeared in 1977, or the one in this book, or perhaps a completely different one?

And why should the order be important? In this new edition each quatrain has been numbered for ease of reference, but what is really new in respect to the previous editions, which contained 122 quatrains, is the fact that now the quatrains have become 123!

When the original version written by Falco Tarassaco was carefully examined, the editor found another quatrain which had gone unnoticed as it was written in a page full of notes. It had been waiting a long time to come to light and almost forty years later this prophecy joins the others, bringing the number to 123.

For the first edition of his prophecies, in September 1977, Falco wrote a short and sibylline introduction in which he said, among other things:

"Their objective [of the prophecies] is to give a hint, some help, or at least to inspire some intuitions immediately after the predictions come true, so "those who understand" can be prepared for what comes next. They have been, therefore, deliberately shuffled, so that only those who study them can understand their mechanism."

Especially during the first years of Damanhur Falco often talked about prophecies. Below are extracts from his lectures on this subject during various meetings he had with fellow researchers, Damanhurians and guests.

"The prophecies of this book are called "Prophecies of the End Times" because these are the last times when many souls want to or must incarnate.

We need to prepare ourselves for a better future. If, for example, the prophecy says that I will drown, I will use the time I have left to learn to swim." (16/01/1979)

"The possibility to obtain time projections is part of the rights of Humankind." (31/03/1988)

"The prophecies were made so someone can use them." (10/05/1988)

"When making a prophecy the prophet is attracted by the strong lights, by those highly emotional and poignant events that, in general, are negative (wars, catastrophes, etc). They are signs which are visible in time. But, the more experienced prophets are able to go beyond these first images and find information for what comes afterward. In order to make a prophecy it is necessary to find the right rhythm-cadence for the divinity. To become tuned in with these forces we must relate with the elements and receive from each one of them the key for access. Every element has its own intelligence and personality; we have to ask that element what is necessary for us to be included in the frame, to go over that threshold – and to make prophecies we must get past five thresholds. The elements represent the thresholds and there is a ritual which allows us to cross these fields.

There is a strong relationship with sounds, because through them human beings can access their ability to make these kinds of time projection, which, please note, are not introspections." (31/03/1988)

"Nostradamus' prophecies are of a special type, as they help calculate times inside the space available to human beings. Unlike, for example, the Book of Revelations where the situations presented, instead of being aimed only at certain individuals – let us say at few elect or other types of people – are more difficult and universal, where the objective is to estimate a sort of end of times. Nostradamus has always been interpreted after the event, because the type of century he uses tends to have the purpose of obtaining measurements inside time. This is the reason why it is considered a book or type of text useful for technicians and those who deal with time matters, in particular with the measure of time, which in magic is always predicted. If we are able to measure time, or use these prophecies in the appropriate manner, we can foresee events of various types and of degree of importance. Above all, though, from these events (which in general concern a large number of individuals in a relatively small geographical area) we can have access, for example, at specific times, to the synchronic lines." (10/05/1988)

"The Prophecies of the End Times" was composed according to two different techniques: one gives a specific time within our era (moreover, this time is relative to the various phases that are connected to one another, for example the periods of thirty years), the other allows us to modify some aspects of certain events that have already taken place in time. I am referring to the possibility of creating parallel existences to pass over specific conditions of time, on a material plane as well. This is a very complex subject though." (31/01/1988)

"The majority of those conditions – if not all of them – are indicated in order to recognize the time when the events take place. Sometimes, these events are not very important but they give the measure of passing time, of the exact point in time where we are. Some of you probably remember a big problem we had in previous years trying to determine the time gap.
We could not ascertain the time we were in and, as a consequence, balancing the events became impossible, we found ourselves in a sort of shipwreck in time. Then, some time ago, the possibility of reconnecting ourselves in time presented itself; we lost our positioning again a couple of times but only for a short period, because it [the positioning] was sufficiently close.

In the coming times, the risk of losing it again will be great, owing to the operations that involve the forces we are dealing with. There, considering everything that is involved, is the risk. Let's hope it will not happen, let's hope we shall have a good enough aim and therefore be able to fix some events that, speaking from an astronomical point of view, are known in terms of time, of date, and are very accurately measured even if they are centuries afar. That will allow us to have a sufficient reference point for all the projections we have made." (December 2, 1991)

Here Falco is referring to two types of prophecies to be found in this book. The first type is represented by those quatrains which make a precise time reference, whereas the others (the majority of them) are supposed to provide elements that enable the creation of another plane of reality or, better still, the ability to monitor how far the new plane of reality, built by Damanhur, is from the original one. The obvious reference here is to the separation of planes described in the introduction.

Let us look at the merits of these two different types of prophecy. The first three quatrains belong to the first group, those that have the function of supplying precise times by which we should have done (and will have to do) things to avoid others.

Quatrains 1, 2 and 3, in fact each contain a mathematical conundrum to solve and understand the three decades that the predictions refer to. After several tries, a solution was found and, for everyone's benefit, today we reveal this with the intention of encouraging every reader to search for solutions for all the many other conundrums contained in the remaining 120 quatrains. Naturally, it would be good if you first tried to solve the first three by yourselves. Have a go…and if you do not succeed then here is the (possible) solution.

Applying Falco Tarassaco's hermetic indications we discover the following.

1. *The "years of great crisis", prophesied in quatrain no.1, would be the years from 1972 to 1980.*

2. *The "years of catastrophe but also of the hope of Aquarius", spoken of in quatrain no. 2, would be the years from 1981 to 1989.*

3. *The years when "there will be no time to think of catastrophes, since all that had been conceived will have begun", spoken of in quatrain no. 3, would belong to the decade from 1990 to around 2000.*

In this way we see that (as Falco stated in his reply on 31/01/1988) the quatrains effectively cover a period of thirty years; in truth it would be exactly thirty years if we stretch the period as far as the year 2002; that year, incidentally, was a very important year for Damanhurians and – from their point of view – for the Planet. This was because it saw the completion of a long and complex ritual process which led to the union between all the friendly Forces of humankind, called the *Triad*. There would only be 28 years in the period if we take it as finishing in 2000, as the solution to the mathematical conundrum of quatrain no. 3 seems to suggest. But this number could be 31 or 32, if we think of closing a cycle respectively at the years 2003 or 2004, years which hold a certain relevance for Damanhurians in virtue of their research on the exploration of time within the framework of Spiritual Physics. Furthermore, there are well documented hypotheses from interpreters of Nostradamus' centuries that would indicate 2004 as a time divide. In either case, if we say "about thirty years" we will not be wrong. In summary, this cycle would span a period starting from the beginning of the seventies to the end of the twentieth century–the beginning of the twenty-first.

Now we are in the year 2016, so are the predictions outdated?

We will reply with three assertions:

- *The quatrains are still relevant.*
- *They touch us closely still, and if we read them carefully we will find references to events that happened well after the year 2000.*
- *They provide the means to guide us in the future.*

These are three important and surprising assertions. Falco Tarassaco himself enlarged on this subject when, in a lecture given in 2009, he was asked to say something more, concerning this cycle of thirty years. He said that once this cycle came to an end it would be repeated. To reinforce this idea Falco, that evening, suggested trying to observe the events following the presumed end of the thirty years cycle. Probably, we would be able to recognize once more the typology of events described in quatrains 1, 2, 3 and in all the others.

He added that after those thirty years had passed, this cycle would once again repeat, and so on.

So this can be seen to be a concrete manifestation of the so called *whirlpools* or *temporal vortices* of which Spiritual Physics[1] speaks with regard to the structure of time in our era and in the immediate future.

1. See *La divinità curiosa*, Val Ra Damanhur, 2007.

Falco also mentioned this in some of his writings, from the theatrical work *The Fourth Ballad* to a series of writings addressed to the Damanhurians, in particular during the eighties.

Again, according to Spiritual Physics, we do not know how long these cycles will recur for, but in any case not longer than the next 600 years. For the Damanhurian esoteric school this period represents a sort of boundary, the end of the line, a barrier beyond which the time structure, as we know it, will start crumbling.

Falco Tarassaco's prophecies describe human, geological, climatic and astronomic events which serve to orientate us in time. We can regroup them under a number of major headings that, for that matter, are common to other well-known prophecies in history. These headings are: deterioration in the customs and habits of humanity in this era, with effects of various kinds on people's mental and physical health; the possibility of a third world war, with the involvement of players from the East and the West; the demise of the present worldwide economic-political system[2]; the end of the line for the Roman Catholic church; a cataclysm able to profoundly alter the geography of the planet; the aftermath of the cataclysm, which would be

2. See Oberto Airaudi (Falco Tarassaco), *Morire per imparare (Dying to Learn)*, in *Il libro del risveglio (The Book of Reawakening,* Italian version only), Val Ra Damanhur, 2004.

characterized (for those still here) by a profound spiritual renaissance; references and suggestions of various types with descriptions of events that are apparently secondary, but probably useful to orientate us in time.

Usually, at this point, most people would say:

"These prophecies are apocalyptic, pessimistic like so many other prophecies, yet the world didn't come to an end on December 21, 2012, like the Mayan prophecies said it would, so they're all just hot air!"

However, that is exactly the reaction that is desired from the masses by those who for so long have been manipulating the meaning of the Mayan prophecies, the Hopi prophecies, the Veda ones, and the prophecies of Nostradamus himself – and we could name more. In fact, the year 2012 was (and is) of great importance because it was (and is) the peak point, astronomically and temporally speaking, which signals the end of one cycle and the beginning of a new one. For the pessimistic we could say that "2012 is when the bad times really start." For the optimistic we would say "2012 marks the irreversible start of a new and better age." Lastly, for those who really want to *"understand"* and really *"do"*, we could cite two simple concepts developed by Falco Tarassaco:

"The prophecies were made so someone can use them."

"We need to prepare ourselves for a better future. If, for example, prophecy says that I will drown, I will use the time I have left to learn to swim."

For readers who wish to study this matter in depth, reading other prophecies can be of great help and a stimulus for further elaboration. Here then is a list of sources that differ greatly one from another, but are of considerable interest:

- *The Hopi prophecies*

- *The Mayan prophecies*

- *The Veda prophecies*

- *The prophecies of the Great Pyramid*

- *The prophecies of Nostradamus*

- *The Prophecies of St.Malachi*

- *The Prophecies of Giordano Bruno*

- *The Apocalypse of John*

- *The Three Secrets of Fatima*

- *The Prophecies of Saint Basil*

- *The Prophecies and Readings of Edgar Cayce.*

- *Certain of Rudolf Steiner's visions*

As a conclusion, we will look at a key for the reading of the events following the year 2000, and the beginning of a new thirty-year cycle in which the prophecies could reveal themselves to be valid again.

We said earlier that the cycle referred to by quatrains 1, 2 and 3 would have ended in the year 2000 or soon after and that the same scheme of events would once again repeat itself. So, we should imagine that this new cycle would begin right after or soon after the close of the previous one. We could venture to say then, maybe somewhat empirically, that the new cycle of thirty years started with the year 2003 or 2004 that it would, like the previous one, last three decades. Now let us return to quatrain no.1 and read it again: this will tell us that the years from 2003 to 2010-2012, approximately, will once again be "years of great crisis".

If we look for validation of this theory and observe the events of the first cycle of thirty years (the decade indicated in quatrain no.1 corresponding to the seventies of the last century) we will note effectively that there was the Great Oil Crisis of 1973 and serious political crisis – think of the *anni di piombo* (years of lead) in Italy.

Let us go forward in time now and ask ourselves if we can apply the formula *"they are years of great crisis"* to the period 2003-2012, that is, to the first decade of the new cycle, as suggested in quatrain no.1. Was there a great crisis again between 2003 and 2012? I leave you to answer…

In the same way, in the spirit of research, we could now try to apply the content of prophecy no.2 (*"they are years of catastrophe"*) to the period 2012-2022/3. Ideas, thoughts, reflections?

Let us then consider the content of quatrain no.3 that states: *"There will be no more time to think of catastrophe, because all that had been pre-arranged will have begun"*; couple this concept with the period around the years 2022(3) - 2033(4).

Time will tell…

"A day will come when humanity will awaken from oblivion and finally realize its true nature and to whom it has given the reins of its existence, to a mind deceitful and mendacious that makes it and keeps it enslaved…humanity has no limits and when one day it realizes this, it will be free even in this world." (Giordano Bruno)

Cigno Banano

DAMANHUR,
FEDERATION OF COMMUNITIES

Damanhur is a Federation of Spiritual Communities in Italy founded in 1974. The first group came to live in Baldissero Canavese, in the province of Turin, in 1979, and has since grown to 25 communities. With just under a thousand people connected to the project, some reside in the communities and others participate more autonomously in research and meditation activities around the world. Damanhur recognizes citizenship to those living in the federation, as well as those who live and support its shared spiritual ideals even while not living in a community. Damanhurians adopt animal and plant names as a symbol of personal renewal through a connection with nature.

Falco Tarassaco, née Oberto Airaudi (philosopher, mystic, healer, writer and painter, 1950 - 2013), was the founder and spiritual leader of Damanhur.

The spiritual philosophy researches contact with the divine matrix of the universe through self-reflection, relations with others, encounters with nature and the study of esoteric traditions of various cultures and peoples. The Damanhurian centers in Italy and in other countries are places of cultural activity and spiritual research, as well as laboratories for artisan works, transformation of food, and much more. The path to spiritual growth encourages the application in daily life—in every expression of human life—of ethical principles characterized by solidarity and sustainability, which can be seen in the many activities in Damanhurian communities and centers.

Damanhurians believe that a spiritual project needs a well-defined organizational structure. For this reason, Damanhur has a written Constitution and the social system includes elected roles, meeting procedures and decisions based on shared rules.

The Federation is an articulated, democratic, highly participatory society active in local politics—presenting electoral lists and engaged in the administration of some local governments. It uses a complementary currency called the "Credito" (credit)—of equal value to the euro—which is even accepted by some local businesses that are not part of Damanhur.

Art in all forms and expressions (music, theater, painting, sculpture...) is considered a tool of self-knowledge and actualization—a way to give voice to the experiences and feelings of all the Damanhurian popolo (population/people).

The Temples of Humankind is the meeting point between art and spirituality. The most well-known work of art at Damanhur, it is a complex of halls and corridors dug by hand (300,175 ft3) completely underground. After digging and building walls, ceilings and floors, Damanhurians have richly decorated each space with mosaics, paintings, glass art and cupulas. The Temples are dedicated to Beauty and Harmony as instruments for the ascension of humanity.

The Federation of Communities invests heavily in hospitality and in welcoming guests to come visit. It is also involved in various academic and university-level research studies.

Damanhur is a member of GEN Europe (Global Ecovillage Network) and RIVE (Rete Italiana Villaggi Ecologici; Italian Network of Ecovillages), who collect the community and eco-living experiences in Italy and beyond, and of CONACREIS (Coordinamento Nazionale Associazioni e Comunitŕ di Ricerca Etica Interiore Spirituale; National Coordination of Associations and Community that Research Ethical Inner Spirituality).

It is possible to get to know Damanhur online, from bookstores, in conferences and courses offered by Damanhurians, and of course, by visiting the Federation in person for a few days or longer.

Damanhur, Federation of Communities
10080 Baldissero C.se (TO) - Italy
www.damanhur.org

Falco Tarassaco, née Oberto Airaudi (1950 - 2013), was the founder and spiritual leader of Damanhur. From childhood, Falco exhibited a precise spiritual vision and a capacity for healing that he developed through constant experimentation outside of traditional, academic institutions. Philosopher, healer, writer and painter, he was an active researcher in the fields of wellness, art and new sciences. Falco's writings had a distinctive philosophical, poetic and esoteric character and have been translated into many languages. As a painter, he gave birth to a field of alchemical painting called, "Selfic painting". His teachings are focused on action, sensibility, exchange with others and positive thinking as tools to discover the divinity hidden inside each one of us.